EMMANUEL JOSEPH

Space Debris and its Impact on Future Space Exploration

Contents

1

Chapter 1: Introduction

Space Debris and Orbital Pollution: The Growing Problem of Space Debris and its Impact on Future Space Exploration

In the vast expanse of the cosmos, human exploration and satellite technology have brought about a remarkable transformation in the way we perceive and interact with the universe. The story of our journey beyond Earth's atmosphere is one of ambition, innovation, and discovery. However, it is also a narrative deeply entwined with a hidden menace that threatens to disrupt our celestial aspirations - space debris.

This chapter serves as an introduction to the critical issue of space debris, a problem that has grown in tandem with our aspirations for space exploration. As we look beyond the stars and consider the possibilities of interstellar travel, colonizing other planets, and reaping the benefits of space-based technologies, it is vital to acknowledge and comprehend the complex issue of space debris.

1.1 The Promise of Space Exploration

Since the inception of the space age with the launch of the Soviet satellite Sputnik in 1957, humanity has embarked on a journey of unprecedented scientific discovery and technological advancement. The exploration of space has not only expanded our understanding of the universe but has also led to practical applications that have transformed life on Earth. Communication satellites have connected people across the globe, Earth-observing satellites have monitored our planet's health, and space missions have reached distant planets and moons.

Space exploration offers us the promise of answering fundamental questions about the cosmos, finding new resources, and providing innovative solutions to the challenges we face on Earth. It has become an integral part of our lives, from GPS navigation to weather forecasting, and from scientific research to national security.

1.2 The Dark Side of Space Exploration

However, the celestial frontier is not without its perils. Among these, the issue of space debris, often referred to as "orbital pollution," has emerged as a formidable challenge. Space debris encompasses a diverse range of human-made objects orbiting Earth, including defunct satellites, discarded rocket stages, and even tiny fragments generated by previous collisions. These objects, large and small, travel at staggering speeds, creating an ever-increasing cloud of potential hazards in low Earth orbit.

1.3 Space Debris Proliferation

The scale of the space debris problem is alarming. Thousands of operational satellites and countless fragments of defunct spacecraft clutter the heavens, traveling at speeds of up to 28,000 kilometers per hour (17,500 miles per hour). The proliferation of space debris poses a direct threat to operational satellites, space missions, and astronauts in orbit. Moreover, the problem is rapidly intensifying as more countries and commercial entities join the space race, launching their own satellites and missions.

1.4 A Call to Awareness

This book, "Space Debris and Orbital Pollution," is a comprehensive exploration of the problem of space debris and its far-reaching implications. Through the following chapters, we will delve into the various aspects of space debris, from its definition and sources to its impact on satellites, the efforts to track and mitigate it, and the global collaborations aimed at solving this problem.

Our journey begins with a call to awareness – to recognize the challenge of space debris and its potential to disrupt our grand aspirations for space exploration. In this modern age of space exploration, the solutions to mitigate and prevent further space debris are not only essential but also an ethical responsibility.

Join us on this exploration of the growing problem of space debris, and let us together chart a course toward a cleaner, safer, and more sustainable cosmos.

2

Chapter 2: Defining Space Debris

2.1 What is Space Debris?

The term "space debris" conjures images of discarded satellites, spent rocket stages, and fragments of defunct spacecraft orbiting Earth. But what exactly is space debris, and how does it differ from natural celestial objects?

Space debris, often referred to as "space junk," is a blanket term for any non-functional human-made objects or fragments thereof, which remain in orbit around the Earth. This definition encompasses a wide array of objects, each with its own story and potential impact. The composition of space debris is diverse, ranging from tiny paint flecks to massive spent rocket stages.

2.2 The Many Faces of Space Debris

Space debris can be categorized into several key types:

2.2.1 Defunct Satellites: These are non-operational satellites that have reached the end of their missions or have malfunctioned. There are thousands of defunct satellites orbiting the Earth, ranging from large communication satellites to smaller scientific probes.

2.2.2 Rocket Stages: After launching a satellite or spacecraft into orbit, the rocket that delivered it becomes space debris. Rocket stages vary in size and are often among the largest debris objects in orbit.

2.2.3 Fragmentation Debris: When two space objects collide, they can produce a cloud of smaller fragments. These fragments are also considered space debris and can pose a significant threat due to their high velocities.

2.2.4 Micro and Millimeter Debris: Even tiny particles, such as flecks of paint, screws, and bolts, can become space debris. Despite their small size, they travel at such high speeds that they can cause damage to operational satellites.

2.3 Sources of Space Debris

Understanding the sources of space debris is essential to tackle the problem effectively. Space debris can be traced back to several key activities:

2.3.1 Launches: Each time a rocket is launched into space, it leaves behind a discarded stage in orbit. As the number of satellite launches has increased, so has the amount of debris created during the launch phase.

2.3.2 In-Orbit Collisions: Collisions between operational satellites, defunct spacecraft, or other debris objects can produce numerous fragments. These collisions are particularly concerning, as they generate new debris that can persist in orbit.

2.3.3 Accidental Explosions: On rare occasions, defunct satellites or rocket stages have exploded in orbit, creating additional fragments and contributing to the space debris population.

2.3.4 Deliberate Debris: Some space missions intentionally release small objects or particles into orbit, which can also become space debris. For example, certain scientific missions release ionized gas to study the Earth's magnetosphere.

2.4 The Growing Challenge

The problem of space debris is intensifying, posing a growing challenge to space exploration and satellite operations. As the number of active satellites, space missions, and launches continues to rise, so does the risk of collisions with existing debris, further adding to the problem.

As we progress through this book, we will explore the impact of this growing menace on satellite operations, space missions, and the long-term sustainability of our activities in space. We will delve deeper into the intricacies of space debris tracking, mitigation strategies, and international efforts to combat this issue.

In the chapters to come, we will unravel the consequences of space debris proliferation and the importance of finding effective solutions to ensure the future of space exploration remains unimpeded by the looming threat of orbital pollution.

3

Chapter 3: The Growing Menace

3.1 Escalating Space Debris Population

As we venture deeper into the problem of space debris, it becomes evident that the issue is far from static; it is dynamic, ever-changing, and escalating. The growing menace of space debris is a direct consequence of the rapid expansion of space activities and the absence of adequate measures to mitigate its proliferation.

The population of space debris in Earth's orbit has been steadily increasing over the decades. The reasons for this growth are multifaceted:

3.1.1 Increased Space Activities: The number of launches and space missions, both by governmental space agencies and private companies, has risen significantly. More objects in space inevitably lead to an increased likelihood of collisions and the generation of new debris.

3.1.2 Collisions and Fragmentation: In-orbit collisions between satellites and debris objects have become more frequent. Each collision produces additional fragments, contributing to the space debris population.

3.1.3 Legacy of Early Space Exploration: The debris created during the early days of space exploration, when regulations and best practices for debris mitigation were less developed, continues to orbit Earth. This legacy debris remains a significant part of the problem.

3.2 Alarming Statistics

To comprehend the magnitude of the growing menace, it is essential to consider some alarming statistics:

3.2.1 Space Trackable Objects: As of the last available data, there were over 20,000 trackable objects in Earth's orbit. These are objects large enough to be tracked by radar and are potential collision risks for operational satellites and spacecraft.

3.2.2 Untrackable Debris: In addition to trackable objects, there are countless smaller fragments and untrackable debris in orbit. These objects are challenging to monitor but can still pose serious threats to space missions and astronauts.

3.2.3 Near Misses: Near-miss incidents, where operational satellites had to perform collision avoidance maneuvers to avoid space debris, have become a common occurrence. These incidents illustrate the imminent danger posed by the growing space debris population.

3.3 Consequences of Proliferation

The increasing number of space debris objects in Earth's orbit has far-reaching consequences. These consequences affect various aspects of space exploration and satellite operations:

3.3.1 Satellite Safety: Operational satellites face a higher risk of collision with space debris, which can disrupt their missions or render them inoperable.

3.3.2 Astronaut Safety: For astronauts aboard the International Space Station (ISS) and future deep-space missions, space debris poses a direct threat to their safety. Evacuation or sheltering measures may be required in the event of a collision warning.

3.3.3 Kessler Syndrome: Coined by NASA scientist Donald J. Kessler, the Kessler Syndrome refers to a hypothetical scenario in which the density of space debris is so high that it leads to a self-sustaining chain reaction of collisions, creating even more debris. This nightmarish scenario could render certain orbits unusable for generations.

3.4 Looking Ahead

As we delve deeper into the complexities of space debris and its impact, it is crucial to recognize the urgency of the issue. The escalating menace of space debris jeopardizes the future of space exploration and satellite operations. Without effective strategies for mitigation and removal, the dream of expanding our presence in space, conducting scientific research, and reaping the benefits of satellite technology could be severely hampered.

In the chapters to come, we will explore various solutions, such as space debris tracking and monitoring, mitigation strategies, and international collaborations, all aimed at addressing the growing problem of space debris and ensuring the continued success and safety of space exploration.

4

Chapter 4: Impact on Satellites

4.1 A Fragile Constellation

Satellites are the unsung heroes of modern life. They enable global communication, weather forecasting, navigation, scientific research, and military operations. However, these invaluable space-based assets are under constant threat from an ever-growing cloud of space debris. In this chapter, we explore the significant impact of space debris on operational satellites.

4.2 Satellites at Risk

Operational satellites orbiting Earth face an imminent danger from space debris. The threat is multi-faceted:

4.2.1 Collisions: Collisions with space debris can cause severe damage or complete destruction of operational satellites. Even small debris fragments can impact at velocities that rival bullets, resulting in catastrophic consequences.

4.2.2 Mission Disruption: To avoid potential collisions, satellite operators often need to maneuver their spacecraft. These maneuvers can consume valuable fuel and reduce the operational lifespan of satellites, leading to financial and operational losses.

4.2.3 Space Traffic Management: The need for frequent collision avoidance maneuvers complicates space traffic management, making it challenging to coordinate and maintain safe orbital paths for satellites.

4.3 The Cost of Replacing and Repairing Satellites

The financial implications of space debris are substantial. The cost of manufacturing, launching, and maintaining satellites is significant, and when a satellite is prematurely lost due to a collision with debris, it incurs not only the financial burden of replacement but also lost revenue and capabilities.

Satellite replacement costs can range from hundreds of millions to billions of dollars, depending on the type and purpose of the satellite. Additionally, the time required to develop and deploy a replacement can leave critical services, such as communication and Earth observation, disrupted.

4.4 The Fragile Web of Connectivity

The impacts of space debris are not isolated. Many aspects of modern life rely on satellite networks, including global telecommunications, internet access, and GPS navigation. Disruptions in satellite services can have far-reaching consequences, affecting sectors such as emergency response, transportation, agriculture, and finance.

4.5 Case Studies

Several incidents serve as poignant reminders of the consequences of space debris on operational satellites:

4.5.1 Iridium 33 and Cosmos 2251: In 2009, the operational Iridium 33 communication satellite collided with the defunct Cosmos 2251 satellite, producing a cloud of fragments that posed immediate threats to other satellites in the same orbital region.

4.5.2 Sentinel-1A Close Call: In 2020, the European Space Agency's Sentinel-1A Earth-observing satellite came within a few hundred meters of a defunct rocket stage, requiring a collision avoidance maneuver to prevent a potential disaster.

4.6 The Need for Mitigation

To safeguard operational satellites and ensure the resilience of satellite services, mitigation efforts are essential. We explore these strategies in detail in subsequent chapters, including the importance of space traffic management, designing spacecraft to be more debris-resistant, and taking proactive measures to reduce the creation of new space debris.

As we move forward in this exploration of space debris and its impacts, we must remember that the consequences of failing to address this problem could extend beyond the realm of space exploration, affecting our everyday lives and the global economy. The satellites orbiting above are vital components of our modern existence, and their protection is paramount in our quest for a cleaner and safer celestial environment.

5

Chapter 5: Space Debris Tracking and Monitoring

5.1 The Watchful Eye of Earth

The safe operation of satellites, space missions, and the International Space Station (ISS) relies on accurate tracking and monitoring of space debris. In this chapter, we delve into the technologies and methods used to keep a watchful eye on the growing population of space debris.

5.2 Radar and Optical Telescopes

Tracking and monitoring space debris involves a combination of ground-based and space-based technologies. Two primary methods are used for this purpose:

5.2.1 Radar Tracking: Ground-based radar stations, such as those operated by the U.S. Space Surveillance Network, emit radar waves to bounce off objects in orbit. By analyzing the return signals, these radar stations can precisely determine the position, velocity, and trajectory of space debris.

5.2.2 Optical Telescopes: Ground-based optical telescopes are used to visually observe and track space debris. These telescopes are equipped with sensitive cameras and are often used for identifying and monitoring specific objects in space.

5.3 Tracking Accuracy

The accuracy of space debris tracking is paramount. Even small deviations in the predicted orbits of debris objects can result in misjudgments regarding potential collisions. To ensure the utmost precision, tracking data is constantly refined, and space debris catalogs are updated regularly.

5.4 Space-Based Tracking

In addition to ground-based tracking, space-based assets are also employed to monitor and track space debris. For example, the ISS is equipped with sensors and cameras that can capture images of nearby space debris. These images are used to track and monitor the movement of debris objects in the vicinity of the station.

5.5 Predictive Models

To avoid collisions and near-misses, predictive models are used to calculate the future positions of space debris objects. These models take into account factors like atmospheric drag, gravitational forces, and any maneuvers conducted by satellites to adjust their orbits. By projecting these factors into the future, predictive models provide crucial information for collision avoidance maneuvers.

5.6 The Challenge of Small Debris

One of the significant challenges in tracking and monitoring space debris is dealing with smaller, untrackable fragments. These tiny particles, often the result of in-orbit collisions, can pose a significant risk to operational satellites and space missions. As of today, tracking such small debris is extremely difficult due to their size and the limitations of current tracking technologies.

5.7 Information Sharing

International cooperation is vital in the sharing of tracking and monitoring data. Organizations such as the U.S. Space Surveillance Network and the European Space Agency's Space Debris Office routinely share tracking information to enhance global space traffic management and collision avoidance efforts.

5.8 The Future of Space Debris Tracking

As the population of space debris continues to grow, the technologies and methods for tracking and monitoring must also evolve. Researchers and space agencies are actively working on innovative solutions, such as improved ground-based radar systems, enhanced space-based tracking sensors, and machine learning algorithms to better predict the movements of space debris.

In the chapters to come, we will explore the crucial strategies for mitigating and removing space debris, as well as the importance of international collaboration in addressing this global challenge. By improving our ability to track and monitor space debris, we take a significant step toward ensuring the safety of our space-based assets and future space exploration endeavors.

6

Chapter 6: Mitigation and Removal Strategies

6.1 A Growing Problem Requiring Solutions

The ever-increasing population of space debris poses a significant threat to satellites, space missions, and the long-term sustainability of space exploration. In this chapter, we explore the strategies and technologies developed to mitigate and remove space debris from Earth's orbit.

6.2 Mitigation Strategies

Mitigation refers to measures taken to prevent the creation of new space debris. While it is challenging to address the existing debris population, focusing on mitigation is critical to prevent further exacerbation of the problem. Several key mitigation strategies have been developed and implemented:

6.2.1 Deorbiting Satellites: At the end of their operational life, satellites are designed to be moved to a lower orbit, where they re-enter Earth's atmosphere and burn up, leaving no debris in orbit.

6.2.2 Passivation: Satellites are designed to minimize the risks they pose after the end of their missions. This includes discharging batteries and venting remaining propellants to reduce the potential for in-orbit explosions.

6.2.3 Collision Avoidance: Satellite operators and space agencies closely monitor orbital paths and adjust satellite trajectories to avoid potential collisions with space debris.

6.3 Active Debris Removal (ADR)

Active debris removal involves the deliberate capture and removal of defunct satellites and large space debris objects from orbit. While this is a complex and costly endeavor, it is seen as a crucial step in addressing the growing space debris problem. Some ADR strategies include:

6.3.1 Harpoon Systems: Harpoons can be used to capture large pieces of space debris, allowing them to be deorbited and safely disposed of in Earth's atmosphere.

6.3.2 Nets and Tethers: Nets and tethers can be used to ensnare space debris, allowing for controlled deorbiting or transportation to a graveyard orbit.

6.3.3 Robotic Arms: Robotic arms or grippers can be attached to spacecraft, enabling them to capture and secure debris objects for removal or safe disposal.

6.4 International Collaboration

Addressing the challenge of space debris necessitates international collaboration. Spacefaring nations, space agencies, and private entities are working together to develop standards, guidelines, and best practices for debris mitigation and removal. Efforts are also underway to establish norms and protocols for active debris removal missions to prevent conflicts and minimize the generation of new debris during removal operations.

6.5 Challenges in Space Debris Mitigation and Removal

The complexities and challenges involved in mitigating and removing space debris are significant:

6.5.1 Cost: Developing and implementing mitigation and removal strategies can be expensive, requiring financial investments from space agencies and the private sector.

6.5.2 Technological Challenges: Designing systems and spacecraft capable of safely capturing and removing space debris is a complex engineering challenge.

6.5.3 Legal and Ethical Considerations: International cooperation requires adherence to legal and ethical guidelines governing space activities, as well as the avoidance of interference with operational satellites.

6.6 The Way Forward

Mitigating and removing space debris is a complex and ongoing endeavor, but it is essential for the long-term sustainability of space exploration and satellite services. As we continue our journey through the following chapters, we will explore space traffic management, the protection of future space missions, and the economic and environmental costs of space debris. By addressing these aspects, we aim to provide a comprehensive view of the challenges and solutions associated with the menace of space debris.

7

Chapter 7: International Collaboration

7.1 A Global Challenge

The issue of space debris is not limited by borders or national boundaries. It is a global challenge that affects all spacefaring nations and has repercussions for the peaceful and sustainable use of outer space. In this chapter, we delve into the vital role of international collaboration in addressing the menace of space debris.

7.2 The Growth of Spacefaring Nations

The early days of space exploration were characterized by the efforts of a handful of major spacefaring nations, primarily the United States and the Soviet Union. However, the space domain has evolved, with numerous countries and even commercial entities actively participating in space activities. This expansion has further heightened the challenges posed by space debris.

7.3 The Need for Coordinated Efforts

As the number of satellites, space missions, and launches continues to grow, so does the complexity of managing space traffic and mitigating the risks associated with space debris. International collaboration is essential for several reasons:

7.3.1 Data Sharing: Collaborative sharing of tracking and monitoring data is crucial to ensure that all space actors have access to comprehensive and accurate information about the location and movement of space debris.

7.3.2 Space Traffic Management: Coordinated space traffic management is essential to prevent collisions and ensure safe orbital pathways for satellites and spacecraft.

7.3.3 Mitigation and Removal Efforts: Efforts to mitigate and remove space debris, such as active debris removal missions, often require international cooperation to avoid conflicts and ensure mission success.

7.4 Key Initiatives

Several key international initiatives and organizations have been established to promote collaboration and address the issue of space debris:

7.4.1 United Nations Committee on the Peaceful Uses of Outer Space (COPUOS): COPUOS plays a significant role in developing international norms and guidelines for space activities, including debris mitigation and space traffic management.

7.4.2 Inter-Agency Space Debris Coordination Committee (IADC): The IADC is a forum for space agencies to coordinate their activities related to space debris. It facilitates data sharing and technical cooperation among member agencies.

7.4.3 European Space Agency's Space Debris Office: The ESA actively monitors and tracks space debris and is engaged in research and efforts related to debris mitigation and removal.

7.5 Collaborative Missions

International collaboration extends to space missions designed to address the space debris problem. For instance, the European Space Agency's e.Deorbit mission is a cooperative project aimed at demonstrating the capture and removal of a defunct satellite in a safe and controlled manner.

7.6 Legal Frameworks

International treaties and agreements also play a crucial role in shaping the norms and rules for space activities, including those related to space debris. The Outer Space Treaty, signed in 1967, sets the foundation for space law and establishes principles such as the peaceful use of outer space, the prevention of harmful contamination, and liability for space activities.

7.7 The Way Forward

As we continue to explore the issue of space debris and its impact on space exploration, it is clear that international collaboration is not just a desirable option but a necessity. The future of space activities depends on the ability of spacefaring nations, organizations, and commercial entities to work together in managing the growing population of space debris and ensuring the safe and sustainable use of outer space. In the upcoming chapters, we will delve into the complexities of space traffic management and the protection of future space missions, both of which rely on robust international cooperation to address this global challenge effectively.

8

Chapter 8: Space Traffic Management

8.1 The Growing Complexity of Space Traffic

The rapid expansion of space activities and the proliferation of space debris have made the management of space traffic an increasingly complex challenge. In this chapter, we explore the importance of effective space traffic management in ensuring the safety and sustainability of space exploration.

8.2 The Basics of Space Traffic Management

Space traffic management involves the coordination, tracking, and regulation of objects in Earth's orbit to avoid collisions and ensure safe and orderly space activities. Key elements of space traffic management include:

8.2.1 Collision Avoidance: Tracking and monitoring space objects to predict potential collisions and conducting maneuvers to prevent them.

8.2.2 Coordination: Ensuring that space actors are aware of each other's activities and orbital paths to avoid conflicts.

8.2.3 Data Sharing: Collaborative data sharing to provide comprehensive information about the location and movement of space objects, including space debris.

8.3 The Role of Space Agencies

Space agencies, such as NASA, ESA, and ROSCOSMOS, play a central role in space traffic management. These agencies are responsible for monitoring and tracking space debris and operational satellites, issuing collision avoidance warnings, and providing coordination among space actors.

8.4 Commercial Space Activities

The rise of commercial space activities, including satellite constellations for communication, Earth observation, and space tourism, has added complexity to space traffic management. Commercial entities are increasingly launching their own satellites and space missions, requiring close coordination with space agencies and other operators.

8.5 Regulatory Frameworks

International agreements and regulatory frameworks are essential for effective space traffic management. Key elements include:

8.5.1 The Outer Space Treaty: Establishing the principles of peaceful use of outer space, cooperation, and the prevention of harmful contamination.

8.5.2 Liability Conventions: Addressing liability issues related to space activities and potential collisions.

8.5.3 Guidelines and Best Practices: The development of guidelines and best practices for space debris mitigation, space traffic management, and coordination among space actors.

8.6 Space Traffic Management Centers

Space traffic management centers, such as the United States Space Surveillance Network and the European Space Agency's Space Debris Office, serve as hubs for tracking and monitoring space objects. These centers provide vital information and support for collision avoidance maneuvers and coordination efforts.

8.7 The Growing Need for Advanced Technology

As the complexity of space traffic management increases, advanced technologies are becoming essential. Radar systems, optical telescopes, and space-based sensors are used to track and monitor space objects. Machine learning and artificial intelligence are also being employed to enhance predictive modeling and collision avoidance capabilities.

8.8 The Way Forward

Space traffic management is an ongoing and evolving discipline. As space activities continue to grow, and as we seek to address the challenges posed by space debris and ensure the sustainability of space exploration, effective space traffic management will be paramount. In the chapters ahead, we will explore the protection of future space missions and the economic and environmental costs of space debris, all of which are closely tied to the successful management of space traffic and the collaborative efforts of spacefaring nations and commercial entities.

9

Chapter 9: Protecting Future Missions

9.1 The Imperative of Protection

As we continue our exploration of the space debris problem and its implications, it is clear that safeguarding future space missions is paramount. In
this chapter, we delve into the strategies and technologies used to protect
spacecraft, satellites, and future missions from the growing menace of space
debris.

9.2 Designing Spacecraft for Resilience

The design of spacecraft and satellites is a critical element of protection
against space debris. Several key principles are employed to enhance
resilience:

9.2.1 Shielding: Spacecraft are often equipped with shielding materials to
protect sensitive components from space debris impacts. These materials
can absorb or deflect debris fragments.

9.2.2 Redundancy: Critical systems are duplicated to ensure mission success
even if some components are damaged by space debris.

9.2.3 Debris-Avoidance Maneuvers: Spacecraft are designed with propulsion systems that enable them to conduct collision avoidance maneuvers when a potential threat is detected.

9.3 Active and Passive Debris Removal

Protection also extends to proactive efforts to reduce the space debris population. Active and passive debris removal strategies are aimed at reducing the risk of collisions for operational satellites and future missions.

9.3.1 Active Debris Removal (ADR): Active removal missions capture and remove defunct satellites and space debris from orbit. These missions help reduce the density of debris in critical orbital regions.

9.3.2 Passive Debris Removal: This strategy focuses on designing spacecraft with components that naturally decay in Earth's atmosphere at the end of their operational life. By ensuring that space objects do not remain in orbit indefinitely, this strategy helps reduce the long-term space debris population.

9.4 Mitigation Measures

Beyond spacecraft design, mitigating the creation of new space debris is crucial for future mission protection. Measures include ensuring that spent rocket stages and defunct satellites are deorbited to burn up in the Earth's atmosphere, thus leaving no debris in orbit.

9.5 Tracking and Early Warning Systems

Space agencies and satellite operators maintain tracking and early warning systems to provide timely alerts about potential collisions with space debris. These systems offer crucial information for conducting collision avoidance maneuvers.

9.6 The Role of Space Traffic Management

The effective coordination and management of space traffic are vital for protecting future missions. Space traffic management centers provide essential support in tracking and monitoring space objects and issuing collision avoidance warnings.

9.7 International Collaboration

The protection of future missions is a global endeavor. International collaboration in space traffic management, data sharing, and mitigation efforts is crucial to ensure the safety and sustainability of space exploration.

9.8 A Holistic Approach

Space debris protection is not limited to any single measure or technology but requires a holistic approach that combines spacecraft design, active and passive debris removal, mitigation efforts, and effective space traffic management. By addressing the challenge from multiple angles, we can protect future missions and continue to explore the cosmos with confidence.

In the upcoming chapters, we will explore the economic and environmental costs of space debris, shedding light on the broader implications of this growing menace and the importance of responsible space activities and stewardship of the celestial environment.

10

Chapter 10: The Cost of Space Debris

10.1 Hidden Costs of Space Debris

While space debris may appear as a remote concern, its economic and environmental impacts are far-reaching and often hidden from view. In this chapter, we delve into the multifaceted costs of space debris and its consequences for space exploration and the world at large.

10.2 Economic Costs

The economic costs of space debris encompass various facets, including:

10.2.1 Satellite Replacement: When operational satellites are damaged or destroyed by collisions with space debris, the financial burden of replacing them can be substantial, ranging from hundreds of millions to billions of dollars.

10.2.2 Repairs and Maintenance: Space agencies and satellite operators spend significant resources on maintaining and repairing satellites that sustain damage from space debris impacts.

10.2.3 Collision Avoidance Maneuvers: Conducting collision avoidance maneuvers to evade space debris can consume valuable fuel, reducing the operational lifespan of satellites and increasing operational costs.

10.2.4 Insurance Premiums: The heightened risk of satellite collisions due to space debris has led to increased insurance premiums for satellite operators, further driving up costs.

10.3 Environmental Costs

The environmental costs of space debris are more subtle but no less significant:

10.3.1 Orbital Pollution: The proliferation of space debris adds to the pollution of Earth's orbital environment, increasing the risk of future collisions and creating long-term challenges for space sustainability.

10.3.2 Spacefaring Nation Responsibility: Spacefaring nations bear a responsibility for the environmental consequences of their space activities, including the generation of space debris.

10.3.3 Space Sustainability: Ensuring the long-term sustainability of space activities is crucial for minimizing the environmental impact of space debris.

10.4 Ethical and Legal Considerations

The economic and environmental costs of space debris underscore the ethical and legal dimensions of the problem:

10.4.1 Ethical Responsibility: Spacefaring nations and commercial entities have an ethical responsibility to address the challenges of space debris and space sustainability.

10.4.2 International Treaties: International agreements, such as the Outer

Space Treaty, set the foundation for space law, including principles of peaceful use, cooperation, and prevention of harmful contamination.

10.4.3 Liability Conventions: Liability conventions govern issues related to space activities, such as collisions and liability for damage caused by space debris.

10.5 Space Stewardship

Effective space stewardship entails responsible and sustainable practices in space activities:

10.5.1 Mitigation Measures: Implementing measures to mitigate the creation of new space debris, such as deorbiting defunct satellites and rocket stages.

10.5.2 Active Debris Removal: Conducting active debris removal missions to reduce the density of space debris in critical orbital regions.

10.5.3 Space Traffic Management: Coordinating space traffic and providing timely collision avoidance warnings to protect operational satellites and future missions.

10.6 The Way Forward

The costs of space debris extend beyond the financial implications and touch on the broader themes of sustainability, ethics, and responsibility. As we continue our journey through the following chapters, we will explore the efforts to mitigate and remove space debris, the challenges of space traffic management, and the protection of future space missions. By addressing these aspects, we aim to provide a comprehensive view of the challenges and solutions associated with the growing menace of space debris.

11

Chapter 11: Toward a Sustainable Future

11.1 The Vision of Space Sustainability

As we approach the conclusion of our exploration of space debris and its multifaceted challenges, it is essential to envision a sustainable future for space activities. In this chapter, we delve into the strategies and initiatives aimed at achieving a cleaner and safer celestial environment.

11.2 The Imperative of Space Sustainability

Space sustainability goes beyond the preservation of the space environment; it encompasses the responsible and ethical use of space for the benefit of all. The imperatives of space sustainability include:

11.2.1 Responsible Stewardship: Spacefaring nations, space agencies, and commercial entities must adopt responsible practices in space activities to minimize the generation of space debris.

11.2.2 Long-Term Vision: A sustainable future in space involves long-term vision and planning to ensure that space activities can continue for generations to come.

11.2.3 Ethical Considerations: Space sustainability is deeply entwined with ethical considerations, including a commitment to cooperation, transparency, and respect for the space environment.

11.3 Space Sustainability Initiatives

Several key initiatives are paving the way toward a more sustainable future in space:

11.3.1 Space Debris Mitigation Guidelines: Space agencies and organizations have developed guidelines and best practices for space debris mitigation, including the deorbiting of defunct satellites and the prevention of in-orbit explosions.

11.3.2 International Collaboration: Collaboration among spacefaring nations is vital for addressing space debris, space traffic management, and the broader goals of space sustainability.

11.3.3 Active Debris Removal Missions: Active debris removal missions, such as the European Space Agency's e.Deorbit mission, are crucial in reducing the density of space debris in key orbital regions.

11.3.4 Transparency and Data Sharing: Providing transparent information and data sharing about space debris and space traffic are fundamental elements of space sustainability.

11.4 Balancing Economic and Environmental Concerns

Achieving space sustainability involves balancing economic interests with environmental concerns:

11.4.1 Responsible Commercial Practices: Commercial entities must embrace responsible practices in space activities, including the management and disposal of defunct satellites.

11.4.2 Incentives for Sustainability: Governments and international bodies can provide incentives and regulations that promote sustainable space activities.

11.5 The Way Forward

The journey toward space sustainability is a collective endeavor that requires the commitment of spacefaring nations, organizations, and commercial entities. By working together to address the challenges posed by space debris and to set the foundations for a sustainable future in space, we can unlock the vast potential of the cosmos for scientific exploration, technological advancement, and the betterment of humanity.

In the concluding chapter of our exploration, we will summarize the key insights and takeaways from this journey through the complexities of space debris, its impact, and the initiatives aimed at securing the future of space exploration and space sustainability.

12

Chapter 12: Conclusion and Key Takeaways

12.1 Reflecting on the Journey

Our journey through the intricate realm of space debris has illuminated the multifaceted challenges and compelling opportunities presented by the growing menace of orbital pollution. As we conclude our exploration, let's reflect on the key takeaways and insights gained from our expedition.

12.2 The Scope of the Problem

Space debris is not a mere inconvenience but a complex and escalating challenge that spans various dimensions:

- Its population continues to grow due to the increasing number of space activities.
  - Collisions and fragmentation events contribute to the space debris population.
  - Even small debris fragments can pose significant risks to satellites, space missions, and astronauts.
  - The long-term environmental costs of space debris are substantial and

require thoughtful consideration.

12.3 Mitigation and Removal Strategies

Addressing the space debris problem involves a combination of mitigation and removal strategies:

- Mitigation strategies aim to prevent the creation of new space debris by deorbiting defunct satellites and rocket stages and avoiding in-orbit explosions.
   - Active debris removal missions, employing technologies like harpoons, nets, and robotic arms, help reduce the density of debris in critical orbital regions.
   - Passive debris removal involves designing spacecraft to naturally decay in Earth's atmosphere at the end of their operational life.

12.4 The Role of International Collaboration

International collaboration is a linchpin in solving the space debris challenge:

- Spacefaring nations, space agencies, and commercial entities must work together to develop standards and guidelines for space debris mitigation and removal.
   - International agreements, including the Outer Space Treaty, set the foundation for space law and responsible space activities.
   - Collaborative efforts in space traffic management and data sharing are vital for space safety and sustainability.

12.5 The Hidden Costs

Space debris has far-reaching economic and environmental costs:

- The financial implications include satellite replacement costs, repairs, maintenance, and increased insurance premiums.

- The environmental costs encompass the pollution of Earth's orbital environment and the responsibility of spacefaring nations.

- Ethical and legal considerations are crucial in addressing the challenges posed by space debris.

12.6 A Vision for Space Sustainability

Space sustainability is the way forward, encompassing responsible stewardship, long-term vision, and ethical considerations:

- Space debris mitigation guidelines and active debris removal missions are essential components of sustainability.

- Space sustainability initiatives involve international collaboration, transparency, and data sharing.

- Balancing economic interests with environmental concerns is key to achieving space sustainability.

12.7 The Collective Journey

Our collective journey through the challenges and opportunities of space debris has provided a panoramic view of the complexities of the space environment. By addressing the menace of space debris and embracing space sustainability, we can continue to explore, innovate, and inspire future generations to reach for the stars.

As we conclude this exploration, let us remain committed to the responsible use of outer space, the protection of our celestial environment, and the enduring quest for knowledge, progress, and discovery in the cosmos. The future of space exploration, free from the looming threat of orbital pollution, is a vision we can achieve through cooperation, innovation, and responsible stewardship.